LET'S THINK
Creatively

Activities to stimulate creative thought processes

Ages 5–11 | Jacqui Arnold

Title:	Let's Think Creatively!
Sub-title:	Activities to stimulate creative thought processes Ages 5-11
Author:	Jacquie Arnold
Editor:	Paula Wagemaker
Designer:	Freshfields Graphic Design
Book Code:	PB00117
ISBN:	978-1-908735-96-6
Published:	2012
Publisher:	TTS Group Ltd Park Lane Business Park Kirkby-in-Ashfield Notts, NG17 9GU Tel: 0800 318 686 Fax: 0800 137 525
Website:	www.tts-shopping.com
Copyright:	Text: © Jacquie Arnold, 2008 Edition and Illustrations: © TTS Group Ltd, 2012
About the author:	Jacquie Arnold has been teaching at various levels of the primary school for the past 10 years. She became interested in thinking skills while studying for her Master of Education degree at the University of Canterbury, Christchurch, New Zealand. During 2001–2002, Jacquie developed and taught a programme for Years 3–6 gifted children. She believes that it is important to implement thinking skills strategies in all areas of the curriculum to encourage children to think for themselves, to question "Why?", and to think "outside the square". She regularly uses her thinking skills activities in mainstream classes.

Photocopy Notice:

Permission is given to schools and teachers who buy this book to reproduce it (and/or any extracts) by photocopying or otherwise, but only for use at their present school. Copies may not be supplied to anyone else or made or used for any other purpose.

CONTENTS

Introduction	**4**
Section One: Originality (Design)	**5**
Teacher Notes	5
Funny Faces	7
Feelings Mask	8
Animal Mix-up	9
A New World	10
Chocolate Treat	11
Wrap It Up!	12
Designer Tree	13
Redesign Your School	14
Scavenger Hunt Board Game	15
Game Time	16
Cartoon Network	17
Superhero for a Day	18
A New Civilisation	19
Playtime	22
Section Two: Originality (Literacy)	**23**
Teacher Notes	23
Story Time	24
Prose Time	25
Silly Sentences	26
Action and Reaction	27
Revamp the Fairytale	28
Rewrite the Ending	29
Designer Party	30
Use Your Senses	31

Section Three: Visualisation	**32**
Teacher Notes	32
Create a Picture	33
Partner Dot Pictures	34
What Can You See?	35
Section Four: Problem-solving	**36**
Teacher Notes	36
Build a House	37
Designer Clothes	38
Redesign Your Bedroom	39
A New Hutch	40
Popcorn Sorter!	41
Boredom Buster	42
Road Trip	43
Create a Toy	44
Designer Cattery	45
Stranded!	46
Create a Gadget	47
CLAD	48
Build a Tower	49
Straw Structure	50
Straw Person	51
Certificates	**52**

INTRODUCTION

Let's Think Creatively! is the second book in a series of three on thinking skills. Links between the three enable you, the teacher, to plan entire lessons or units using activities from the books.

This second book contains activities that encourage children to think of new ideas and new ways of doing things, to think outside the square, and to look at the world they live in through new eyes. The activities also foster in children a desire to ask "Why?" or "Why not?" rather than to accept what they see or hear.

To maintain the focus on creativity, activities emphasise:

- **Originality:** Using imagination and innovation to create new ideas and methods to accomplish tasks
- **Visualisation:** Creating pictures and ideas in the mind
- **Problem-solving:** Discovering or investigating solutions to problems.

I have grouped the activities in this resource into four sections that cover each of these attributes. Two of the sections are given over to different aspects of originality. Teacher notes at the beginning of each section briefly outline the primary purpose of the activities within that section, set out teaching points, and, in some cases, offer ideas for extension activities. The latter are designed to extend the pupils on a particular skill or theme, but I have left it to you to decide how they should be used (e.g., for early finishers or with the entire class or group). You will also find, at the very end of the book, a series of certificates that you can photocopy and distribute to the children.

The worksheets encompass a variety of curriculum areas, and I have trialled many of the activities the sheets contain in creative writing and classroom reading programmes. You can therefore use the activities in this book as part of a thinking skills programme or integrate them into your daily mainstream classroom programme. You can also use some of the activities as starter or evaluation activities for particular topics and/or as one-off learning experiences.

I have designed many of the worksheets as master sheets so that you can reuse them or adapt them to reinforce learning. Because learning styles (visual, auditory, tactile, and kinaesthetic) play an important role in how children learn, I have annotated each worksheet with the learning styles that the activity encompasses and the main objectives of the anticipated learning experience. I have also indicated on each sheet the level(s) of the primary school for which the activity is best suited.

Unless I specify otherwise in the text, the children can work on the worksheets individually, in pairs, in groups, or as a whole class, as you see fit. The levels indicated on each worksheet are guidelines only, which means you can modify activities to suit the needs and levels of your pupils.

Overall, the key purpose of this book is for you and your pupils to have fun with creativity—to experiment with ideas and new ways of doing things, to think "What if . . .?" and to explore the outcomes, and to recognise the endless possibilities that lie within each creative thought or idea.

SECTION ONE:

Originality (Design)

TEACHER NOTES

Purpose
The following activities encourage pupils to use their imagination and innovation to create new ideas through drawing and design.

General Teaching Points
- Encourage imagination, thinking outside the square, and innovation rather than accuracy of drawings.
- Pupils can work on activities individually, in pairs, or in small groups, depending on their age levels and abilities.
- Set time limits for each activity. However, pupils may need several opportunities to refine or redo some designs and activities.
- Give pupils the freedom to express ideas that in other settings might be considered ridiculous or attract ridicule from their peers.
- Some pupils may need encouragement and extending to promote creative thinking. Rather than directing the pupils, ask open-ended questions, such as "What else could you do?"
- You can run some of the activities as units of work, for example, "Superhero for a Day" and "A New Civilisation".

Teaching Points for Specific Activities
- **New World:** Show pupils photos and/or paintings of landscapes and discuss the colours evident for each feature within them. This process ensures all pupils are aware of the concept of a landscape and will help them understand what the activity requires of them. Remove the pictures before you introduce the activity, as some pupils may try to imitate them.
- **Cartoon Network:** Show examples of cartoons to the class that emulate the type of cartoon you wish the pupils to develop. Teach the basic concepts and layouts of cartoons.
- **Wrap It Up!:** Provide examples of packaging used for other food items and discuss the requirements of effective packaging (colours, wording, bar codes, ingredients, etc).
- **Redesign Your School:** Take the pupils for a walk around the school, asking them to note all features. Then, with the class, draw a map of the current layout of the school to ensure pupils are aware of map layout and proportions. Pupils do not need to follow this layout, but can start afresh with their new designs.
- **Playtime:** Visit the playground at your school or local park. Discuss its features. Discuss with the class features they might find at theme parks or sports parks, etc. Ensure pupils are aware that they can be as creative as they like—the only criterion is that their playground has to fit into a specified area at their house.

Extension

Animal Mix-up
- One partner chooses the animal body parts for the other partner to combine to create a new animal.
- Increase the number of animal body parts to be included.

A New World
- Pupils create models of the "new worlds", using available materials (tactile).

Wrap It Up!
- Pupils create a poster advertising their new chocolate bars.

Designer Tree
- Pupils create models of their trees, using available materials (tactile).
- Pupils write a paragraph stating why their trees are special and how they would benefit the world.

Redesign Your School
- Pupils make models of their new schools, using available materials (tactile).

- Pupils design a new curriculum for their new schools.

Cartoon Network
- Pupils draw a short humorous comic strip with their new character in it.

Superhero for a Day
- The pupils each:
- Create their superhero costumes either for themselves or for a model (e.g., an action doll) (tactile).
- Create a model of their superhero's transportation, using available materials (tactile).
- Design an appropriate residence for their superhero. They draw and label all features of the residence and explain why they have included these features.
- Create a model of their superhero's residence, using available materials (tactile).
- Present their design and/or models to the class or the members of a group.

A New Civilisation
- Pupils make a model of their island, using available materials (tactile).
- Pupils create their national costume, using paper, and model it to the class or members of a group (tactile).
- Pupils create their national food dish, using real ingredients, and then ask the class or the members of their group to sample it.

Playtime
- Pupils build a model of their playground, using available materials (tactile).
- Pupils present their design and/or model to the group or class.

Funny Faces

Draw a different "funny" face in each of the shapes below. You can add as many features as you like to make each face look humorous.

Present your "faces" to a partner or group.

LEVEL:	FOCUS:	LEARNING STYLES:
KS 1	Originality	Visual, Auditory

Worksheet

Feelings Mask

☺ How are you feeling today? In the box below, design and draw a full face mask that you could wear to show how you are feeling.

☺ Using materials available in your classroom, construct your mask and then decorate it.

☺ Display your mask to your class. Can they guess how you are feeling?

LEVEL:	FOCUS:	LEARNING STYLES:
KS 1	Originality	Visual, Auditory, Tactile

Animal Mix-up

🌀 Choose six animals. Choose ONE part of the body from each animal (e.g., head, legs, tail, hide, nose, ears, main part of body). Create a new animal by combining your chosen SIX animal body parts. Draw your animal in the box below. Give your animal a new species name.

Name:

🌀 Present your new animal to a partner, group, or the class.

LEVEL:	FOCUS:	LEARNING STYLES:
KS 1	Originality	Visual, Auditory

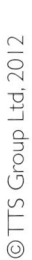

Worksheet

A New World

🌀 If you had created the world, what colour would you have made the following features of our world?

Feature	Colour
Sky	
Clouds	
Sea	
Rocks and stones	
Leaves on trees	
Grass	

Feature	Colour
Sun	
Rivers	
Mountains	
Tree trunks	
Flowers	
Bees	

🌀 Are there any other features you would like to change colour? List them here.

🌀 Using the colour(s) you chose, draw a picture of your newly coloured world in the box below.

LEVEL:	FOCUS:	LEARNING STYLES:
KS 1	Originality	Visual

Chocolate Treat

⊚ Create a new chocolate bar that you would love to eat.

- What flavour or flavours of chocolate would you use in your bar?

  _____ _____

  _____ _____

- What other ingredients would you put in your chocolate bar?

  _____ _____

  _____ _____

- What will be the size and shape of your new chocolate bar?

  _____ _____

  _____ _____

⊚ Draw your new chocolate bar below, making sure you label all the main ingredients. Give your chocolate bar a name.

[   ]

The name of my chocolate bar is: _____

⊚ Using dough, make a real-size model of your chocolate bar. Paint your model.

⊚ Present your chocolate bar to a small group or the class. Tell them why your chocolate bar is the best chocolate bar in the world.

LEVEL:	FOCUS:	LEARNING STYLES:
KS 1 & Lower KS 2	Originality	Visual, Auditory, Tactile

Worksheet

Wrap It Up!

- Using the chocolate bar you created in Chocolate Treat, design an appealing wrapper for your bar. Think carefully about the colours and words that you will use on your wrapper. Remember to include any other necessary information on your wrapper design.

- Draw a rough copy of your design below. Show what colour you want each part to be. You do not need to colour this design in completely.

- Once you are happy with your design, create a life-size wrapper for your chocolate bar, using available materials. Enclose the dough model of your chocolate bar in the wrapper.

- Present your new chocolate bar to a partner or group.

LEVEL:	FOCUS:	LEARNING STYLES:
Lower KS 2	Originality	Visual, Auditory. Tactile

Designer Tree

🌀 Create and design a new unique and imaginative tree. You will need to consider the following attributes:

- The height of your tree
- The type of bark on your tree
- The "fruit" your tree will produce (colour, taste, size)
- The trunk of your tree
- The leaves on your tree (colour, shape, size)
- The seed of your tree (colour, shape, size)
- The best conditions for your tree to grow in.

🌀 Draw your tree in the box below, labelling all of the above features. Record any necessary details on your diagram.

LEVEL:	FOCUS:	LEARNING STYLES:
Lower KS 2	Originality	Visual

Worksheet

Redesign Your School

- Think about the layout of your school. How many classrooms are there? Do you have a library or a hall? What other buildings are there? Does your school have playgrounds, playing fields, a wildlife area, etc?

- Redesign your school. Include as many new features as you think would be necessary to create your ideal school. Be imaginative and creative. You have an unlimited budget. Draw a map of your new school design below. Think carefully about the placement and size of all your buildings, playgrounds, and any other features that you consider important. Remember to label all features or to provide a key.

LEVEL:	FOCUS:	LEARNING STYLES:
Upper KS 2	Originality	Visual

Scavenger Hunt Board Game

🌀 Go on a scavenger hunt in an area specified by your teacher (e.g., the school playground, a garden, the beach). Collect the following items.

> One item that is:
> - round
> - rectangular
> - brown
> - green
> - soft
> - hard
> - made of plastic
> - made of wood

🌀 Using the eight items that you found on your scavenger hunt, design and construct a 3D board game for children aged 8 to 10 years.

- You may use additional paper, cardboard, glue, etc. Ensure your game is appealing to look at, easy to use, and interesting to play.
- Give your game a name.
- Write a set of rules for your game. Remember to specify how many players can play at one time.
- Play your game with a partner.
- Are there any changes you need to make to your game to improve it? Replay the game when you have made these changes.

🌀 Fill in the evaluation chart below. Score each criterion on a scale of 1 to 5, with 1 meaning "not at all" and 5 meaning "definitely".

	Self-evaluation	Partner evaluation
Game is appealing to look at		
Game is easy to use		
Game is interesting to play		

LEVEL:	FOCUS:	LEARNING STYLES:
KS 1 & 2	Originality	Visual, Auditory, Tactile

Worksheet

Game Time

◎ Create a new outdoors team game or sport for your class to play. You can combine parts of well-known games or sports, create a completely new game, or do a combination of both. If you base your new game or sport on known games or sports, take only ONE rule or part from each (minimum five games or sports). Your game needs to be enjoyable and simple to play.

◎ Fill in the Team Game Planning Guide below by answering the following questions:
- What will you call your new team game or sport?
- What equipment will you need to play your new game or sport?
- How many teams do you need to play your game?
- How many people should there be in each team?
- How will you play your game?
- What formation do you require to play your game?

◎ On separate paper, draw a diagram showing the area you need, any markings, and the set-up of the teams and equipment. Make sure your instructions and rules clearly explain step by step how to play the game. Consider if your game has time limits, a system for scoring points, and a referee. Write on the back of your sheet if necessary.

Team Game Planning Guide

Name: _____

Equipment: _____

Teams: _____

Game Set-up: _____

Rules: _____

◎ Play your game with your class. Revise any unclear instructions. If necessary, write in additional instructions. Modify any parts of your game that did not work as you intended. Are there any other improvements you could make? Play your game again and then assess it by using ticks to answer the following questions. Ask one of your classmates to answer the questions too.

Game Assessment	Self Yes	Self No	Peer Yes	Peer No
Was the game enjoyable to play?				
Were the instructions easy to follow?				
Was the game simple to play?				

LEVEL: Upper KS 2 FOCUS: Originality LEARNING STYLES: Visual, Auditory, Kinaesthetic

© TTS Group Ltd, 2012

Cartoon Network

🌀 Create a new cartoon character that will star in a prime-time cartoon series for children. The series is a comedy based on everyday life and it will be screened on television from Monday to Friday at 8.00 a.m. Your cartoon character needs to be humorous and to appeal to both boys and girls five to seven years of age. Your character can be a fictional one. Be as creative as you like.

🌀 Design and draw your new cartoon character below. Give your character a name.

Name:

🌀 Present your work to a group or the class.

LEVEL:	FOCUS:	LEARNING STYLES:
Upper KS 2	Originality	Visual, Auditory

Worksheet

Superhero for a Day

🌀 Imagine that you are a superhero for one day—a superhero who has never been seen on earth before but who will benefit the world today in some way.

🌀 List the superpowers that you would have. State how your superhero powers could help the world today.

• Superpowers: _____

• How my superhero would help: _____

🌀 Design a costume for your superhero in the box opposite. Include all the equipment that he or she would need. Label all accessories and features, and explain why you believe these are necessary. Give your superhero a name.

🌀 In the box below, design an appropriate form of transport for yourself as a superhero. Label all the features and equipment that you would need. Give your design a title and explain why this form of transport is appropriate and beneficial.

The name of my superhero is:

_____

Title: _____

Explanation: _____
_____

LEVEL:	FOCUS:	LEARNING STYLES:
Upper KS 2	Originality	Visual, Auditory, Tactile

A New Civilisation

Page One of Three

🌀 You have discovered an island that no one has ever discovered or lived on before. You decide to set up a new civilisation on your island.

ISLAND FACTS

Area: 50 square kilometres

Geography: Golden sandy beaches, rocky headlands
Small mountains in the middle
Sloping flat lands down to the sea
Covered in tropical jungle, including tropical fruit trees
Two large rivers running from the mountains down to the sea

Climate: Temperature range 20°–30°C (depending on season)
High rainfall during "winter" period
Eastern side of island prone to strong sea winds

🌀 On a large piece of paper, draw a map of your island, remembering to include all of the features listed above. You may add extra features to your island. Indicate where North is on your map and use a key. Choose a name for your island and write the name at the top of your map.

🌀 Determine on your map where you will build two towns. Mark your towns on your map and name them.

🌀 What materials will you use to build the houses in your towns?

🌀 Decide where you will develop a port for ships. Mark and name your port on your map.

🌀 What forms of transport will there be on your island?

🌀 Draw any necessary "roads" on your map. Make sure that these will allow easy access between the towns, port, and any other features that you consider important. The nature of your "roads" will depend on the form of transport you have chosen.

LEVEL:	FOCUS:	LEARNING STYLES:
Upper KS 2	Originality	Visual, Auditory, Tactile

Worksheet

🌀 Create your own alphabet for your civilisation. Once you have decided on the number of letters in your alphabet, write or draw your choices in the boxes below.

🌀 Write a list of 30 important words in your new language. Ensure that you provide the meaning of each word.

Word	Meaning	Word	Meaning

LEVEL: Upper KS 2
FOCUS: Originality
LEARNING STYLES: Visual, Auditory, Tactile

◎ In the space below, design a national costume that is unique to your island. This costume will be worn on special occasions.

◎ Create a national food dish for which your island will become famous. This dish will be served on special occasions. Choose a name for your new recipe and list the key ingredients.

- Name: _____

- Ingredients:

◎ Present your new civilisation to a partner, group, or the class.

LEVEL:	FOCUS:	LEARNING STYLES:
Upper KS 2	Originality	Visual, Auditory, Tactile

21

Worksheet

Playtime

Design an ultimate adventure playground for you to play in at your house. Decide if your playground will be an inside or an outside playground. Choose the features (minimum of FIVE) your playground would need to have to make it your ultimate adventure playground. Draw your design below, labelling all features. Think carefully about the size and structure of your playground. Underneath your design, state where your playground is to be built.

- My playground will be built _____

LEVEL:	FOCUS:	LEARNING STYLES:
KS 1 & 2	Originality	Visual, Auditory

SECTION TWO:
Originality (Literacy)

TEACHER NOTES

Purpose
The activities in this section encourage pupils to use their imagination and innovation to produce and expand on new ideas and ways of thinking when using literacy-based activities. Many of these activities can be used as part of a creative writing or reading programme.

Teaching Points
- Encourage imagination and originality. The focus is not on realistic or rational ideas, but on creative and divergent thinking.
- Pupils need to have the freedom to express ideas without fear of ridicule from their peers.
- With "Revamp the Fairytale", you may need to choose the fairytale. You may also find it necessary to work through a tale as a model before the pupils attempt this activity individually.

Extension

Story Time and Prose Time
- Each pupil asks a partner to write down a list of unrelated words and then uses these words to write a story.

Silly Sentences
- Pupils work in pairs. One pupil writes down four unrelated words. The other pupil writes a sentence using these words.

Action and Reaction
- Pupils work in pairs. One pupil writes the fortunate events and the other pupil writes the unfortunate events.

Designer Party
- The pupils, as a class, design and hold a class party that celebrates the five senses.

Story Time

Write a story that includes all of the following words. You can use the words in any order.

- dog
- cow
- house
- sat
- cake
- book

Share your story with a partner.

LEVEL:	FOCUS:	LEARNING STYLES:
KS 1	Originality	Visual, Auditory

Prose Time

Compose a poem or story that includes all of the following words. You can use the words in any order.

- bat
- rat
- mat
- freeze
- breeze
- leaves
- frown
- crown
- down

Share your poem or story with a partner.

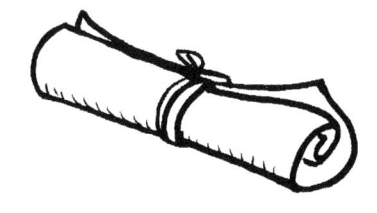

LEVEL:	FOCUS:	LEARNING STYLES:
Lower KS 2	Originality	Visual, Auditory

Silly Sentences

Write a sentence for each of the following lists, using all of the words provided.

dog	log	frog	bog

car	bar	far	tar

rake	wire	bird	hot

tractor	cut	mouse	mud

mountain	leaf	water	cat

boat	ring	foot	camel

sand	candle	horse	box

LEVEL: KS 2 FOCUS: Originality LEARNING STYLES: Visual, Auditory

Action and Reaction

Complete the following story by continuing the pattern of fortunate events and unfortunate events. Each event needs to influence the next event. Try to finish your story with a fortunate event.

- **One morning I leaped out of bed. Unfortunately, I tripped over the cat. Fortunately, I landed on a soft cushion. Unfortunately,**

Share your story with a partner or group.

LEVEL:	FOCUS:	LEARNING STYLES:
Upper KS 2	Originality	Visual, Auditory

Worksheet
Revamp the Fairytale

☺ Choose a fairytale. Write its title above the boxes below.

☺ Think of a new ending for your chosen fairytale. Draw a sequence of pictures in the four boxes below to show how you think the fairytale should end. Write one sentence underneath each picture to describe what is happening.

Title: _____

Sentence:

Sentence:

Sentence:

Sentence:

☺ Share your new ending with a partner or group.

LEVEL:	FOCUS:	LEARNING STYLES:
KS 1	Originality	Visual, Auditory

Rewrite the Ending

- Choose a story (e.g., fairy tale, picture book, novel) where you did not like the way the story ended. Perhaps the ending was sad, unrealistic, or left questions unanswered, or perhaps you just did not like what happened.

- Write the title of your chosen story below and the original author if known. Rewrite the ending of your chosen story (minimum of 10 sentences) to conclude the story in the way that you would have liked it to end.

Title: _____   Author: _____

- Share your new story ending with a partner or group.

LEVEL:	FOCUS:	LEARNING STYLES:
KS 2	Originality	Visual, Auditory

Worksheet

Designer Party

◎ Consider your five senses—sight, smell, hearing, taste, and touch.

◎ Design a birthday party that will provide an exciting experience for each of your five senses. Choose a theme for your party and record at least one idea beside each of the senses below.

Birthday Party Theme: _____

Your Birthday Age: _____

Sense	Idea
Sight	
Smell	
Hearing	
Taste	
Touch	

◎ Share your ideas with a partner.

LEVEL:	FOCUS:	LEARNING STYLES:
KS 1 & 2	Originality	Visual, Auditory

Use Your Senses

- Use your five senses (sight, smell, hearing, taste, and touch) to plan an event, trip, or celebration.

- Choose an event, trip, or celebration and write it here:
  _____

- Record an appropriate experience for each of the five senses listed below that will ensure your event, trip, or celebration is successful.

Sense	Experience
Sight	
Smell	
Hearing	
Taste	
Touch	

- Share your ideas with a partner or group.

LEVEL:	FOCUS:	LEARNING STYLES:
KS 2	Originality	Visual, Auditory

SECTION THREE:

Visualisation

TEACHER NOTES

Purpose
The activities in this section encourage pupils to visualise a picture based on the stimuli provided. You can use these activities as stand-alone creativity activities or integrate them into art or maths lessons.

General Teaching Points
- Focus on the creative visualisation and imagination of each pupil rather than on their drawing accuracy.
- A suitable warm-up for these activities is to ask pupils to find shapes or pictures in the clouds in the sky. Ask the class to lie down or sit outside and observe the clouds. What shapes or pictures of objects, things, animals, and so on, can they see?
- Give pupils the freedom to draw whatever they visualise.
- You can repeat these activities over numerous occasions.

Teaching Points for Specific Activities
- **Partner Dot Pictures:** Encourage pupils to space out dots over the entire box rather than group them together.
- **What Can You See?:** Encourage pupils to draw large initial "shapes" for their partners.

Extension
- Place restrictions on and set topics for what the pupils have to draw. For example, in "Create a Picture", possible topics are Animals, Transport, and Objects.

Create a Picture
- Ask the pupils to work in pairs, taking turns to draw between the dots. Tell them they are not to discuss with each other what they are drawing.

Partner Dot Pictures
- Increase or decrease the number of dots each pupil must draw.
- Have each pupil draw a specified number of dots (e.g., 20) in the box and then give the page to a partner, who will create a picture using the dots.

Create a Picture

Draw lines between each of the dots below to create a picture of an object, person, or animal. Each dot can connect with no more than two other dots. You must use all of the dots in your picture. Give your picture a title.

Title: _____

LEVEL:	FOCUS:	LEARNING STYLES:
KS 1 & 2	Originality, Visualisation	Visual, Auditory

Worksheet

Partner Dot Pictures

Work with a partner. Each of you draws 15 dots in the box below.

Taking turns, draw lines between each of the dots you both made to create a picture. You must use all of the dots in your picture. You may use each dot more than once. Give your picture a title.

LEVEL:	FOCUS:	LEARNING STYLES:
KS 1 & 2	Originality, Visualisation	Visual, Auditory

What Can You See?

○ Work with a partner. Ask your partner to draw a shape on a piece of paper. The shape can be any shape at all, with any number of sides, but its ends must meet. In the space below, and using the shape your partner has drawn, create a picture of an animal, object, or person. Give your picture a title.

Title:

○ Ask your partner to draw a continuous line in the space below. The line can follow any pattern but the ends must not meet. Using the line your partner has drawn, create a picture of an animal, object, or person. Give your picture a title.

Title:

LEVEL:	FOCUS:	LEARNING STYLES:
KS 1 & 2	Originality, Visualisation	Visual

SECTION FOUR:

Problem-solving

TEACHER NOTES

Purpose
The aim of the following activities is to enable pupils to discover, work towards, design, and/or investigate a solution to a problem. Many of these activities cater for all four learning styles.

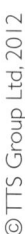

Teaching Points
- Outline or revisit problem-solving techniques before setting the activities. For example:
  - Identify the problem to be solved.
  - Determine what factors and requirements need to be considered and/or met to solve the problem.
  - Decide if there is any other information required and where to locate this information.
  - Pose possible solutions.
  - Trial the solution and then refine or redesign as necessary.
- Finding your way through a maze is an analogy that you can use when describing the process of problem-solving to pupils. Pupils need to be aware that an unsuccessful solution does not indicate failure, merely one pathway that led to a "dead-end" and that, as such, it is still an important step in the process of finding a solution to the problem. Pupils also need to determine any successful elements of this solution, and reapply, adapt, or start over to create a new solution.
- Your role is to act as a facilitator by ensuring pupils follow the problem-solving process successfully, by posing appropriate questions, and by guiding them towards appropriate resources and lines of thought.
- The pupils can complete the activities individually, in pairs, or small groups, depending on their age levels and capabilities.
- Set time limits for each activity. However, pupils may need opportunities to trial, refine, or redo designs as they seek solutions to the problems and so may benefit from working on the activity over a number of days.
- Ensure pupils have the freedom to express ideas without fear of ridicule from their peers.

Extension

Redesign Your Bedroom
- Pupils construct a model of their new bedroom, using available materials (tactile). They then present their designs and/or models to the members of their group or to the class.

The New Hutch
- Pupils design a poster advertising the benefits of their rabbit hutch.
- Pupils construct a model of their rabbit hutch, using available materials (tactile).

Create a Toy
- Pupils design an advertising brochure for their new toy detailing why it is a "must have" toy for every five- and six-year-old child.
- Pupils create their toy, using available materials (tactile).

Designer Cattery
- Pupils design a poster that advertises the benefits a cat will experience when staying at their cattery.

Build a House

You have found a tiny person in your garden. This person is only 10 centimetres tall. You decide to build your new friend a house that will keep him or her dry, warm, and safe.

- Using available materials, design and construct a home for your new friend. Consider carefully what your new friend's house will need (e.g., the number of rooms, windows, doors). You will need to take into consideration the size of your friend. You will also need to design and construct furniture for your new friend.

- Use the space below to draw your designs before you start any construction.

LEVEL: KS 1

FOCUS: Originality, Problem-solving

LEARNING STYLES: Visual, Tactile

Worksheet

Designer Clothes

You have discovered a tiny person in your garden who is only 10 centimetres tall. Your new friend has only one set of clothes.

🌀 Give your new tiny friend a name.

🌀 Design and draw below a set of new winter clothes for your friend that will keep him or her warm.

My friend's name is: _____

🌀 Using paper, material, wool, etc, create the clothes you designed. Think carefully about what size the clothes will need to be to fit your friend.

🌀 Set up a fashion display in your classroom.

LEVEL:	FOCUS:	LEARNING STYLES:
KS 1	Originality, Problem-solving	Visual, Tactile

Redesign Your Bedroom

🌀 Redesign your bedroom to become the ultimate living space of the century. You can be as creative as you like.

> Your ultimate living space needs to:
> - Include sleeping facilities
> - Be fully self-contained in case of an emergency (e.g., flood, earthquake)
> - Include any other feature(s) that you consider necessary.

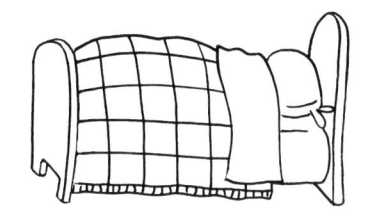

🌀 Draw a floor plan of your new bedroom. Your diagram will need a title, key, and explanations as to why you have included at least FIVE accessories or features.

Title: _____

Key: _____

🌀 Share your design with a partner or small group.

LEVEL:	FOCUS:	LEARNING STYLES:
Lower KS 2	Problem-solving	Visual, Auditory

Worksheet

A New Hutch

🌀 Design a new rabbit hutch for a pet rabbit or guinea pig that you can sell in veterinary shops.

Your hutch must include:
- A sleeping area
- Food and water containers
- A waterproof area
- An area for grass and plants
- Activities to keep the pet rabbit or guinea pig fit
- Activities to entertain the pet rabbit or guinea pig.

🌀 Draw your design below, remembering to label all the parts.

🌀 Share your design with a partner or small group.

LEVEL:	FOCUS:	LEARNING STYLES:
Lower KS 2	Originality, Problem Solving	Visual, Auditory

Popcorn Sorter!

Every Friday night, the Smith family watches a film together. Mum or Dad always makes popcorn using the popcorn maker. The Smiths like to watch the film in the dark. However, as some kernels of corn will not pop, the Smiths need to have the lights on when they are eating their popcorn to avoid eating those hard bits.

- Design a simple popcorn sorter for the Smith family that would separate the cooked popcorn from the kernels that have not popped, so allowing the Smith family to eat their popcorn in the dark. Consider carefully the materials you will need to construct your sorter.

- Draw your design below. Label all the materials you will need, and list the equipment you will need to build it.

Equipment:

- Construct your popcorn sorter.

- Test your popcorn sorter.

LEVEL: Lower KS 2

FOCUS: Problem-solving

LEARNING STYLES: Visual, Auditory, Tactile

Worksheet

Boredom Buster

You have broken both of your arms. Your arms are in casts up to your shoulders. You can only move your arms up and down and side to side, and you can only touch your thumb and first finger together on each hand. To relieve the boredom, you decide to read a book. However, you find it very difficult holding the book and turning the pages.

- Design and construct a holder that will hold up the book for you to read. You must be able to touch the pages.

- Next, design and construct a page-turner that will help you to turn the pages of the book.

- Carefully consider the materials you will need for both items. Use the spaces below to draw your designs before constructing the holder and the page-turner.

Holder

Page-turner

- Test your holder and page-turner.

- Present them to a group or the class.

LEVEL:	FOCUS:	LEARNING STYLES:
Lower KS 2	Problem-solving	Visual, Auditory, Tactile

Road Trip

You are going by car on a trip that will take eight hours. Redesign your seat in your car to include at least TEN new features and accessories that will keep you occupied during the journey.

Write down the new features and accessories below and explain why you have chosen to include these.

Features and Accessories	Explanation
1.	
2.	
3.	
4.	
5.	
6.	
7.	
8.	
9.	
10.	

Draw a picture of your seat with its new features and accessories. Include labels on your diagram.

LEVEL: Lower KS 2

FOCUS: Problem-solving

LEARNING STYLES: Visual

Worksheet

Create a Toy

Create a new toy, which has the following features.

The toy must:
- Appeal to a five- to six-year-old boy and/or girl
- Be unique
- Have moveable parts
- Make a sound
- Be childproof
- Be educational in some way.

Draw the design of your new toy in the box below. Give your design a name. Label all its features.

The name of my toy is:

LEVEL: KS 2

FOCUS: Originality, Problem-solving

LEARNING STYLES: Visual, Auditory

Designer Cattery

You have been employed to design the rooms for a new cattery where cat owners will leave their precious cats when they go away on holiday. You have been given an unlimited budget.

🌀 Write down what you think cat owners would expect and want a cattery to have.

🌀 Write down what you think a cat would want or need a cattery to have.

🌀 Now draw below your design for a room in a cattery to house a cat. Your room must cater for all the needs and wants of both the cat owner and the cat that you listed above. Label all features.

LEVEL:	FOCUS:	LEARNING STYLES:
Upper KS 2	Problem-solving	Visual

Worksheet

Stranded!

You are stranded in a small boat in the middle of an ocean in a storm. The sails for the boat were swept away by a strong gust of wind, which also broke the mast and sent it overboard. You can see land far away in the distance. On board the boat, you have:

- A picnic backpack complete with cutlery (knives, forks, and spoons, plates, and cups for four people)
- A small chopping board
- A picnic rug
- Two metres of rope
- A pocket knife.

You have enough food and water to last you for two days.

⊙ In order to survive, you need to design the following, using only the materials that are available on your boat:

- A shelter on the boat that will protect you from the storm.
- A new "oar" that will enable you to paddle back to shore. Unfortunately, you have broken one of your ribs and cannot lean over the side of the boat to paddle.

⊙ Draw your designs below. Label all materials used.

⊙ Present your work to a group or the class.

LEVEL:	FOCUS:	LEARNING STYLES:
Upper KS 2	Problem-solving	Visual, Auditory

Create a Gadget

You decide to build a gadget that will allow you to reach out and pick up items off your desk and your bookshelf while lying down on your bed. The catch is that you have to make the gadget from items found in a kitchen.

Your bedroom measures three metres by three metres. Your bed is one metre in width, your desk is 50 centimetres wide, and your bookcase is 25 centimetres wide. Your bed stands against one wall and your bookcase and desk stand against the parallel wall.

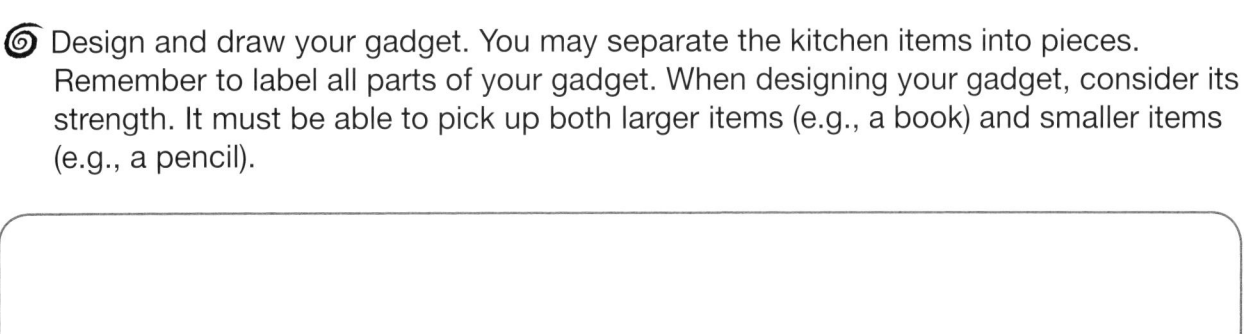

- Design and draw your gadget. You may separate the kitchen items into pieces. Remember to label all parts of your gadget. When designing your gadget, consider its strength. It must be able to pick up both larger items (e.g., a book) and smaller items (e.g., a pencil).

LEVEL:	FOCUS:	LEARNING STYLES:
Upper KS 2	Problem-solving	Visual

Worksheet

CLAD

Use the CLAD (**C**hange, **L**engthen, **A**dd, **D**ecrease) technique to modify and improve an object, animal, or person. Be as creative as you like. Draw each alteration in the appropriate space and write underneath why you think this modification will be an improvement. Once you have made a change, you cannot alter that feature again.

◎ Draw the object, animal, or person that you want to modify here:

Change
Remove one feature and add a new feature

C

This will be an improvement because:

Lengthen
Make one feature longer or bigger

L

This will be an improvement because:

Add
Add a new feature

A

This will be an improvement because:

Decrease
Reduce one feature in size

D

This will be an improvement because:

◎ Share your work with a partner.

LEVEL:	FOCUS:	LEARNING STYLES:
KS 2	Problem-solving	Visual, Auditory

Build a Tower

◎ Working in small groups, use blocks, rods, or any other construction equipment to build a tall tower.

- You have a time limit of 30 minutes to complete your tower.
- Your tower must meet the following criteria:
  - Be completed within the time limit
  - Able to support a closed picture book of any size on top without falling down
  - Remain standing after a "Puff Test" (three people blowing at the same time on the tower from a specified spot).

◎ At the end of the 30 minutes, measure the height of your tower, and then test your tower according to the above criteria. Using the table below, record your results and the results of other teams, using a √ or x where appropriate.

Criteria	Results				
	Team A	Team B	Team C	Team D	Team E
Building materials used					
Completed within time limit					
Tower height (centimetres)					
Holds a picture book on top					
Passed "Puff Test"					

◎ Compare the results for each team's tower. Did any of the results surprise you? Why?

LEVEL: KS 1

FOCUS: Problem-solving

LEARNING STYLES: Tactile, Auditory, Kinaesthetic

Worksheet

Straw Structure

Working in small groups and using only straws, build a structure that will hold an open picture book at least 10 centimetres off a table. You may use scissors. You cannot use any form of adhesive (e.g., glue, tape, string, etc.) to hold your structure together.

- You have a time limit of 30 minutes to complete your structure.
- Your structure must meet the following criteria:
  - Be completed within the time limit
  - Not be put together with adhesives
  - Able to hold an open picture book of any size
  - Able to hold the picture book 10 centimetres off the table at each corner
  - Able to remain standing after a "Puff Test" *(three people blowing at the same time on the structure from a specified spot).*

At the end of the 30 minutes, test your structure according to the above criteria. Using the table below, record your results and the results of other teams below with a √ or x.

Criteria	Results				
	Team A	Team B	Team C	Team D	Team E
Completed within time limit					
No adhesives used					
Holds an open picture book					
Holds picture book 10 centimetres off the table					
Passed "Puff Test"					

LEVEL: Lower KS 2

FOCUS: Problem-solving

LEARNING STYLES: Visual, Auditory, Tactile, Kinaesthetic

Straw Person

🌀 Using only straws, construct a model of a person.

- Your model must meet the following criteria:
  - Measure 15 centimetres or more in height
  - Be fully clothed (clothes to be made from straws)
  - Able to stand by itself.

🌀 Use your imagination and be as creative as you like. Use the straws in any way that you wish to construct your model. You may use scissors, but you cannot use glue or any other form of adhesive.

🌀 Give your person a name.

🌀 At the end of 45 minutes, test your model, using the above criteria. Record your results below, using a √ or x.

My straw person is named: _____

Criteria	Results				
	Team A	Team B	Team C	Team D	Team E
Completed within time limit					
Measures 15 centimetres or more					
Fully clothed					
Able to stand by itself					
Constructed of straws only					

LEVEL:	FOCUS:	LEARNING STYLES:
Upper KS 2	Originality, Problem-solving	Visual, Auditory, Tactile, Kinaesthetic

You are an Awesome CREATIVE THINKER!

DATE   SIGNED

You are an Amazing PROBLEM-SOLVER!

DATE   SIGNED

SUPERB CREATIVITY!

DATE   SIGNED

Outstanding skill in PROBLEM-SOLVING!

DATE   SIGNED

Great originality of THOUGHT!

DATE   SIGNED

Excellent PROBLEM-SOLVING SKILLS!

DATE   SIGNED